Rock kids

A journal for kids to record their rock and mineral discoveries

This Rock Log belongs to:

First of all, thanks to the Great Rock Creator for the diversity and beauty of rocks and minerals. Wow. Also, thanks to Cathy, Paul, and Kari, our North Shore rockhound buddies and forever friends!

De: I'm grateful to my husband Pete, parents Marilyn and Ralph, and sons Mike and Dan, for their support. Special thanks to Dan, also my co-author, for putting up with my book-writing process.

Dan: I'd like to thank my mom for encouraging me to be curious about rocks and my brother for joining me in all the rock-hunting adventures. Dad waited for us and dealt with reduced m.p.g. every time we filled our vehicle with multiple pails of rocks that took hours to collect, thanks!

This book wouldn't have happened without the support and encouragement of Brett and the crew at AdventureKEEN—a million thanks! Special gratitude to Gerri and Gordon Slabaugh, who decided to accept the first logbook 20 years ago!

Cover and interior design/illustration:
DeAnna Brandt, Daniel Brandt
Content: DeAnna Brandt, Daniel Brandt

10 9 8 7 6 5 4 3

Published by:
Adventure Publications
An imprint of AdventureKEEN
(800) 678-7006
www.adventurepublications.net

Printed and bound in China

ISBN 978-1-59193-777-7 (pbk.)

Notice: The information contained in this book is true, complete, and accurate to the best of our knowledge.

All recommendations and suggestions are made without any guarantees on the part of the authors or Adventure Publications.

The authors and publisher disclaim all liability incurred in connection with the use of this information.

Neither the publisher nor the authors shall be liable for any damage which may be caused or sustained as a result of the conduct of any of the activities in this book.

Reference photos of cover rock and coloring rocks by Renee Kirchner, many thanks.

What's a Rock?

To understand rocks, you've got to know what a mineral is first. A mineral is a chemical that has hardened (crystallized) into a specific shape; each mineral is made up of its own unique recipe of chemicals. For example, sand is made up of a combination of silicon and oxygen.

Rocks are made up of more than one mineral. The Earth's crust is made of rock. That includes everything from mountains to the bottom of the oceans! There are three basic groups of rocks, and they all formed in different ways. They are: igneous, sedimentary, and metamorphic.

Igneous Rock

Igneous rocks form when molten rock (rock that's so hot it melts) cools down. There are two ways this can happen. Magma, which is the word for molten rock within the Earth, cools down slowly, allowing crystals to develop slowly before it is eventually exposed on Earth. Such rocks are called intrusive rocks. Granite is one example of this kind of igneous rock. It is famous for being "shiny" and having many crystals. The other kind of igneous rock (known as extrusive rock) forms when molten rock erupts from a volcano and is exposed to air or water, usually cooling too fast to produce visible crystals.

Some types of igneous rock: granite, obsidian, and basalt.

Sedimentary Rock

Sedimentary rocks form when sediment (tiny parts of rocks, minerals, or chemicals) develops in layers, which then harden over time, turning to stone.

Some types of sedimentary rock: limestone (made of tiny shells of ocean life), sandstone, flint, and chalk.

Metamorphic Rock

Metamorphic rocks form when igneous or sedimentary rocks are exposed to the great pressure and heat inside the Earth. This squishes the rocks and causes them to change.

Types of metamorphic rock: marble, soapstone, schist, and slate/gneiss.

Rock Cycle

Over millions (and sometimes billions) of years, rocks form, erode, and are destroyed. This is called the Rock Cycle. Heat and pressure, melting and cooling, weathering and erosion, compacting and cementing are all things that can create or change a rock.

- **Igneous rocks** are created when a volcano erupts and the lava or magma cools down and hardens.

- When an igneous or metamorphic rock is worn down by rain, wind, or bumping around in streams, it breaks down into small pieces called sediment. The sediment is crushed and forms a layer, eventually becoming **sedimentary rock.**

- When an igneous or sedimentary rock gets slowly buried deep underground, it gets hot and is squished, eventually changing into a **metamorphic rock.**

- When a metamorphic rock breaks down on the surface, it can create the sediment necessary to make sedimentary rock. Metamorphic rocks can also melt, becoming an **igneous rock** when it cools, either on the surface or within the Earth. **The rock cycle never ends.**

A Summary of the Rock Cycle

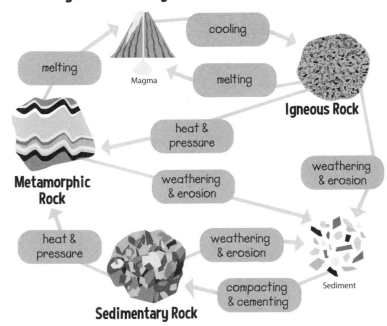

cooling

melting

melting

Magma

Igneous Rock

heat & pressure

weathering & erosion

Metamorphic Rock

weathering & erosion

heat & pressure

weathering & erosion

Sediment

compacting & cementing

Sedimentary Rock

What's a Mineral?

A mineral is a specific chemical that has hardened into a solid form (called a crystal). Every mineral has its own unique recipe (called a chemical formula). Those recipes are made up of chemical elements, the basic building blocks of nature.

- Each mineral has its own chemical recipe, and the entire mineral is made out of it. Salt is a mineral, and it's entirely made up of a combination of sodium and chlorine. Because minerals are made up of the same material, you can test them for hardness and streak (the color they make when scratched). A rock is made of many different minerals, so it has many individual chemical recipes in it and can't be tested in this way.

- Common minerals include quartz, salt, and feldspar. Other minerals you may know are agate, ruby, diamond, copper, gold, silver, emerald, iron ore (hematite), amethyst (purple quartz), and turquoise. There are around 3000 to 4000 different minerals on Earth.

Friedrich Mohs, a German scientist, designed a scale to help figure out how hard minerals are. **The Mohs Scale of Hardness** is what most people use to measure a mineral's hardness. A 1 on the scale is softest and a 10 is the hardest.

HARDNESS	MINERAL
1	Talc
2	Gypsum
3	Calcite
4	Fluorite
5	Apatite
6	Feldspar
7	Quartz
8	Topaz
9	Corundum
10	Diamond

HARDNESS	EVERYDAY ITEM
2.5	Fingernail
3	Copper Penny
4	Nail
5.5	Window Glass
6.5	Steel Knife Blade

Everyday Rocks and Minerals

- **Electricity:** Electricity moves through certain metals (such as copper) very easily, which is why wiring and other items that use electricity all contain copper.

- **Food, Soap, and Cleaners:** The mineral salt is used in food, to melt ice on the street in winter, and in many soaps and cleaners too.

- **Cooking Pots, Silverware, Appliances, Tools:** Stainless steel is made of steel (a combination of iron, carbon, and other materials), and chromium. Unlike steel or iron, it doesn't rust, so it's used to make cookware, silverware, and appliances. Dentists and doctors use special tools made of stainless steel.

- **Matches, Fireworks, Batteries, Fertilizer, Bath:** Sulfur is a mineral used in matches, fireworks, batteries, and fertilizer. Some people soak in hot springs that contain natural sulfur.

- **Paper, Pencils:** Most paper is made of wood and minerals (talc, bentonite, sometimes mica and clay). Lead pencils, despite their name, are made with graphite and clay, not lead!

- **LED Light Bulbs:** There are about 18 minerals in an LED light! Here is a partial list: gold, silver, arsenic, copper, lead, silica, zinc, boron, limestone, tin, bauxite, barite, manganese, gallium, indium, and selenium.

- **Cement, Bricks, Flower Pots:** Clay is made of super-tiny grains of various minerals and used in bricks, flowerpots, and as an ingredient in concrete. Many people use clay to make pottery.

- **Drinking Glasses, Window Glass:** Glass is mostly made of quartz. Pure quartz sand is melted down and mixed with other ingredients to make glass in different sizes, shapes, and colors.

- **Soda/Pop Cans:** Bauxite is a sedimentary rock and the main source of the mineral aluminum. Aluminum is lightweight, doesn't rust, and can be molded easily to any shape.

State Rocks

In all, 46 states in the U.S. have chosen a state rock, mineral, gemstone, or fossil. Some of them also have a state metal and more! Check out your own state below.

Alabama
Hematite, Marble, Star Blue Quartz

Alaska
Gold, Jade

Arizona
Copper, Turquoise, Petrified Wood

Arkansas
Quartz Crystal, Bauxite, Diamond

California
Gold, Serpentine, Benitoite

Colorado
Rhodochrosite, Yule Marble, Aquamarine

Connecticut
Garnet

Delaware
Sillimanite

Florida
Agatized Coral, Moonstone

Georgia
Staurolite, Quartz

Hawaii
Black Coral

Idaho
Idaho Star Garnet

Illinois
Fluorite

Indiana
Salem Limestone

Iowa
Geode

Kentucky
Coal, Kentucky Agate, Freshwater Pearl

Louisiana
Lapearlite

Maine
Tourmaline

Maryland
Patuxent River Stone

Massachusetts
Babingtonite, Rhodonite, Roxbury Puddingstone

Michigan
Petoskey Stone, Isle Royale Greenstone

Minnesota
Lake Superior Agate

Mississippi
Petrified Wood

Missouri
Galena, Mozarkite

Montana
Sapphire, Montana Agate

Nebraska
Prairie Agate, Blue Chalcedony

Nevada
Black Fire Opal, Sandstone, Nevada Turquoise, Silver

New Hampshire
Smoky Quartz, Granite, Beryl

New Mexico
Turquoise

New York
Garnet

North Carolina
Gold, Granite, Emerald

Ohio
Ohio Flint

Oklahoma
Barite Rose

Oregon
Thunder Egg, Oregon Sunstone

Rhode Island
Bowenite, Cumberlandite

South Carolina
Blue Granite, Amethyst

South Dakota
Rose Quartz, Fairburn Agate

Tennessee
Tennessee Paint Agate, Tennessee River Pearl, Limestone

Texas
Petrified Palmwood, Texas Blue Topaz, Silver

Utah
Copper, Coal, Topaz

Vermont
Talc, Marble, Granite, Slate, Grossular Garnet

Virginia
Nelsonite

Washington
Petrified Wood

West Virginia
Bituminous Coal, Mississippian Fossil Coral

Wisconsin
Galena, Red Granite

Wyoming
Wyoming Nephrite, Jade

Famous Rocks

There are many spectacular natural rock formations or man-made buildings that incorporate rocks and minerals. Here is a peek at a few of them. Look them up online or in the library, and if you can, go visit!

Hawai'i Volcanoes National Park—Hawaii

This national park has two active volcanoes: Kilauea, one of the most active volcanoes on Earth, and Mauna Loa, an absolutely massive volcano. At the park, you can get views of active lava flows and hike across recently cooled lava. Many rare birds, animals, and plants are found here too.

Wawheap Hoodoos—Utah

A hoodoo is a large column of soft rock covered by a "cap" of harder rock. The Wawheap Hoodoos are huge white columns of 160-million-year-old Entrada sandstone, capped by 100-million-year-old Dakota sandstone, and they are incredible to see!

Antelope Canyon—Arizona

Antelope Canyon is a visually stunning pair of slot canyons of sandstone which formed due to water erosion. Light beams (or "shafts") in both canyons are a photographer's dream!

Carlsbad Caverns—New Mexico

Known as the "Grand Canyon with a roof on it," Carlsbad Caverns are limestone caves containing crazy cave formations, including huge crystals and stalactites/stalagmites. Over 119 caves are in the park.

Stonehenge—England

This prehistoric monument is a circle of standing stones. The largest one is 27 feet tall; some of the stones weigh more than 35 tons but were moved by hand (or by boat) over 4000 years ago.

The Pyramids at Giza—Egypt

Huge buildings that served as tombs for kings, the three largest pyramids required millions of very heavy blocks of limestone to create.

Giant's Causeway—Northern Ireland

The 40,000 basalt columns found here formed from lava as it cooled, although some residents once claimed the columns were built by giants. Most columns are hexagonal (six-sided), and the tallest reach nearly 39 feet.

Common Words

Agate: A special form of chalcedony that is famous for its beautiful lines of colors

Amethyst: A purple form of quartz that is a popular collectible

Band: A line of color on a rock; some gemstones, such as agates, have many colorful bands on them

Basalt: An igneous rock that forms when lava cools down very quickly

Calcite: A soft, often white mineral that contains the element calcium; it is very common and is one of the first minerals young rock collectors should learn to recognize

Chalk: A variety of limestone that is made up of the tiny shells of long-dead ocean life

Copper: A metal famous for its use in coins (especially older pennies), electronics, and statues; copper is actually an element

Diamond: A very hard form of the element carbon

Element: One of the building blocks of nature; there are 118 elements in all; everything in the world is made up of some mix of elements

Flint: A kind of quartz that has been used to make tools (and start fires) for tens of thousands of years

Fool's gold: Another name for pyrite, a golden mineral that is sometimes mistaken for gold

Fossil: The remnants of a long-dead animal that are preserved when conditions are just right

Fracture: How a rock tends to break when hit by an object

Fulgurite: A special rock that's made when lightning strikes sand, melting it and producing a sand-covered glass tube

Geode: A hollow, ball-like rock that looks normal but contains crystals inside it; these are often sold at rock shops and tourist sites

Gneiss: A metamorphic rock that formed when granite (or other rocks) were put under a large amount of heat and pressure; pronounced "nice"

Granite: An igneous rock that formed deep within the Earth; granite is well known for its visible crystals

Graphite: A gray, soft mineral that is made out of carbon; you might not realize it, but you've already held graphite—it's the "lead" in your pencil

Hardness: When it comes to rocks, hardness refers to how easy it is to scratch a mineral; there's even a scale to help you know how hard a mineral is: the Moh's Hardness Scale. It goes from 1 to 10; a mineral of 1, like talc, is so soft you can scratch it with your fingernail. A 10, like diamond, is so hard that nothing (except for another diamond) will scratch it. Knowing how hard something is can help you know what you've found

Igneous rock: Rock that formed when lava or magma from a volcano cooled

Lava: Molten rock that is on the Earth's surface

Magma: Molten rock that is still inside the Earth; when it reaches the surface, it's called lava

Marble: A metamorphic rock often used in buildings, decorations, and art

Metamorphic: Rock subjected to heat and pressure deep within the Earth, changing it into different rock entirely

Meteorite: A rock that falls from space, entering the Earth's atmosphere and landing on the ground; most space rocks burn up in the atmosphere, and they are known as "meteors" or "shooting stars"

Mineral: A mix of chemicals that have crystallized, taking on a solid form

Ore: A rock that is mined for the metal that it contains

Pearly: Having a pearl-like shine

Peat: The remnants of wetland plants that were never fully broken down, creating a thick material that is related to coal

Petrified wood: Ancient trees whose wood was replaced by stone, creating stone trees that perfectly resemble the original plants

Pyrite: A golden mineral that is famous for its bright gold color; see "fool's gold"

Quartz: A combination of silicon and oxygen, quartz is the most common mineral in the world and also a popular collectible

Rock: A combination of minerals; there are three kinds of rocks: igneous, sedimentary, and metamorphic. Igneous rocks formed when molten rock cooled; sedimentary rocks were gradually deposited over time in layers; metamorphic rocks formed when existing rocks were exposed to great amounts of heat and pressure

Sediment: Material that settles in layers, such as sand at the bottom of the ocean, or dirt or mud in a field

Sedimentary rock: Rock that formed when layers of sediment hardened; for example, mudstone formed when layers of mud hardened; limestone sometimes formed when the remains of dead animals formed layers and hardened

Silica: A combination of the elements silicon and oxygen; sand is made of silica, and so is quartz, the most common mineral on Earth

Rock Display Box

There are many ways to display your growing rock/mineral collection. Use a tackle box, jewelry box, egg carton, or other container with small, separate compartments.

- Create labels from paper strips to fit in each compartment. On the label, write the type of rock/mineral, and the date and location where you found or bought it. Use colorful pens, pencils, or fine-point markers.

- Line each bottom section with a stretched-out cotton ball, tissue paper, or piece of fabric.

YOU CAN MAKE YOUR OWN DISPLAY by starting with a shoebox, or recycle a cardboard box from most any store (free if you ask).

Supplies needed: a box, stiff cardboard, scissors, marker, paper, and cotton balls or fabric.

- Cut the box down (ask an adult for help with this) to make it short—about 1½-2 inches deep.

- For a 2-inch-deep box, cut stiff cardboard strips 2 inches wide and long enough to reach from side to side inside the box. Then cut more 2-inch strips that are long enough to reach from the top to the bottom inside the box.

- Take all the newly cut strips, and figure out how many compartments you want and what size. Create a grid with the strips. Where they intersect, cut 1-inch slits on each strip so they slot together (see diagram below).

- Line the bottom and label each compartment.

- Clean your best rock/mineral specimens with water and an old toothbrush. Let them dry and then display them!

10

Log Tips

Rock Hunting

When hunting for rocks/minerals, bring along this **Rock Log** and something to write with. A camera and magnifying glass are both useful but not necessary. Bring a bag/backpack to put the rocks in that you collect (ask an adult if it's okay), a bottle of water to keep you hydrated, sturdy shoes, and a hat and sunscreen to keep you safe from the sun.

Record It

As you explore, fill out a **Log** page with information about the rock or mineral that you have found and draw a picture of it. If it is allowed (ask an adult), keep the rock for your collection. Identify what kind of rock/mineral it is using a field guide, a rock book, or using the internet to find out more about it.

You can record up to 30 rocks/minerals on your **Life List**. Transfer the dates and rock/mineral types from the **Log** pages to your **Life List** pages to create a quick view of your progress.

Have Fun!

Learn more with the rock/mineral **Facts** and explore and play games with the **Activities**, all located on the right side of the **Log** pages.

Be Creative!

There is more space to draw directly onto the **Photos/Art** pages, or attach your original artwork, a photo you've taken, a postcard, or a picture from a magazine.

Respect Nature

Please leave rocks/minerals where you find them if on private land or publicly protected property. Before collecting anything, ask an adult if it's okay. State and national parks have their own rules about what you can take from their property. Stay with an adult, and always ask permission before going onto private land.

Stay Safe!

Rock hunting in pits and on the edges of roads, highways, or roof-tops is not safe. Also use caution when rock hunting in or near streams, creeks, rivers, and lakes.

Other Uses

You don't have to be outside to use this log. Bring this **Rock Log** and something to write with to a science museum or a natural history museum, watch a show on TV, or go online to check out more about rocks/minerals.

Life List

	Date	Rock/Mineral
1		
2		
3		
4		
5		
6		
7		
8		
9		
10		
11		
12		
13		
14		
15		

Life List

Date	Rock/Mineral
16	
17	
18	
19	
20	
21	
22	
23	
24	
25	
26	
27	
28	
29	
30	

Log

Date/Time:_____

City/State:_____

Rock location (in/near): ☐ lake ☐ mountain
☐ forest ☐ desert ☐ stream/river/creek
☐ other_____

Shape: ☐ mostly round ☐ mostly jagged
☐ other_____

Size: ☐ pea ☐ grape ☐ golf ball
☐ tennis ball ☐ larger or smaller, describe:
_____

Look/feel (check all that apply): ☐ rough
☐ smooth ☐ crystals ☐ banded ☐ veins
☐ layers ☐ pebbled ☐ grainy ☐ flaky
☐ holes/pockets ☐ other_____

Mostly metallic or metallic flecks/veins? If so,
describe:_____
_____

Color(s):_____
_____

Dull or shiny/glassy? Describe:_____
_____

Transparent or opaque? Describe:_____
_____

Type of rock/mineral I saw (enter this on your Life List)

Are there more of the same rock nearby?____

Describe the surrounding rocks/minerals:____

_____

_____

What I did with the rock: ☐ put it back
☐ saved for collection ☐ saved to give away

Other interesting things I noticed:

_____

_____

_____

_____

It looks like this (drawing or photo):

Fact

MOUNT RUSHMORE: ONE LARGE CARVING!

Located in South Dakota, Mount Rushmore is a huge granite sculpture featuring the faces of former U.S. Presidents George Washington, Thomas Jefferson, Theodore Roosevelt and Abraham Lincoln. Each face is 60 feet tall, and it took more than 14 years for Gutzon Borglum, his son Lincoln, and 400 workers to complete the sculpture. Workers used a number of tools to carve the igneous rock: from dynamite and jackhammers to small hammers and chisels. Today the site draws more than three million people each year.

Log

Date/Time:_____

City/State:_____

Rock location (in/near): ☐ lake ☐ mountain
☐ forest ☐ desert ☐ stream/river/creek
☐ other_____

Shape: ☐ mostly round ☐ mostly jagged
☐ other_____

Size: ☐ pea ☐ grape ☐ golf ball
☐ tennis ball ☐ larger or smaller, describe:
_____

Look/feel (check all that apply): ☐ rough
☐ smooth ☐ crystals ☐ banded ☐ veins
☐ layers ☐ pebbled ☐ grainy ☐ flaky
☐ holes/pockets ☐ other_____

Mostly metallic or metallic flecks/veins? If so,
describe:_____
_____

Color(s):_____
_____

Dull or shiny/glassy? Describe:_____
_____

Transparent or opaque? Describe:_____
_____

Type of rock/mineral I saw (enter this on your Life List)

Are there more of the same rock nearby?____
Describe the surrounding rocks/minerals:____

_____

_____

What I did with the rock: ☐ put it back
☐ saved for collection ☐ saved to give away

Other interesting things I noticed:

_____

_____

_____

_____

It looks like this (drawing or photo):

Fact

THE "SAILING STONES" OF DEATH VALLEY

At a dry lake bed in Death Valley National Park, large stones were spotted with trails behind them, as if they had been pushed along. Over time, the rocks moved again. Scientists knew from the park staff that people weren't moving the stones, but no one knew why they were moving. As it turned out, a meltwater pond froze overnight, then started to melt, creating sheets of ice. With some wind, the ice became battering rams that pushed the rocks along!

Log

Date/Time:_____

City/State:_____

Rock location (in/near): ☐ lake ☐ mountain
☐ forest ☐ desert ☐ stream/river/creek
☐ other_____

Shape: ☐ mostly round ☐ mostly jagged
☐ other_____

Size: ☐ pea ☐ grape ☐ golf ball
☐ tennis ball ☐ larger or smaller, describe:
_____

Look/feel (check all that apply): ☐ rough
☐ smooth ☐ crystals ☐ banded ☐ veins
☐ layers ☐ pebbled ☐ grainy ☐ flaky
☐ holes/pockets ☐ other_____

Mostly metallic or metallic flecks/veins? If so,
describe:_____
_____

Color(s):_____
_____

Dull or shiny/glassy? Describe:_____
_____

Transparent or opaque? Describe:_____
_____

Type of rock/mineral I saw (enter this on your Life List)

Are there more of the same rock nearby?____

Describe the surrounding rocks/minerals:____

_____

_____

What I did with the rock: ☐ put it back
☐ saved for collection   ☐ saved to give away

Other interesting things I noticed:

_____

_____

_____

_____

It looks like this (drawing or photo):

Activity

ROCK SKIPPING

Also called rock skimming, the current world record is 88 skips by an American man.

Scientists have tested and discovered the best way to skip a rock: Choose a smooth oval stone, with a weight and size that fits in your hand well.

Then, hold the rock at a 20-degree angle in your hand and throw it hard at a 20-degree angle into the water.

With practice, you should be able to skip your rocks many times and make them go really far!

Log

Date/Time:_____

City/State:_____

Rock location (in/near): ☐ lake ☐ mountain
☐ forest ☐ desert ☐ stream/river/creek
☐ other_____

Shape: ☐ mostly round ☐ mostly jagged
☐ other_____

Size: ☐ pea ☐ grape ☐ golf ball
☐ tennis ball ☐ larger or smaller, describe:
_____

Look/feel (check all that apply): ☐ rough
☐ smooth ☐ crystals ☐ banded ☐ veins
☐ layers ☐ pebbled ☐ grainy ☐ flaky
☐ holes/pockets ☐ other_____

Mostly metallic or metallic flecks/veins? If so,
describe:_____
_____

Color(s):_____
_____

Dull or shiny/glassy? Describe:_____
_____

Transparent or opaque? Describe:_____
_____

Type of rock/mineral I saw (enter this on your Life List)

Are there more of the same rock nearby?____

Describe the surrounding rocks/minerals:____

_____

_____

What I did with the rock: ☐ put it back
☐ saved for collection ☐ saved to give away

Other interesting things I noticed:

_____

_____

_____

_____

It looks like this (drawing or photo):

Fact

FROM PLANTS AND TREES TO COAL

Coal is a sedimentary rock that started out as a plant. Bogs, swamps, and other areas contain a lot of decaying plants and plant material. Over time, those plants die and form layers at the bottom of the bog, eventually creating a thick spongy material called peat. Over millions of years, the peat hardens, becoming coal, a black rock that is one of the most common fuels on Earth.

Log

Date/Time:_____

City/State:_____

Rock location (in/near): ☐ lake ☐ mountain
☐ forest ☐ desert ☐ stream/river/creek
☐ other_____

Shape: ☐ mostly round ☐ mostly jagged
☐ other_____

Size: ☐ pea ☐ grape ☐ golf ball
☐ tennis ball ☐ larger or smaller, describe:
_____

Look/feel (check all that apply): ☐ rough
☐ smooth ☐ crystals ☐ banded ☐ veins
☐ layers ☐ pebbled ☐ grainy ☐ flaky
☐ holes/pockets ☐ other_____

Mostly metallic or metallic flecks/veins? If so,
describe:_____
_____

Color(s):_____
_____

Dull or shiny/glassy? Describe:_____
_____

Transparent or opaque? Describe:_____
_____

Type of rock/mineral I saw (enter this on your Life List)

Are there more of the same rock nearby?____

Describe the surrounding rocks/minerals:____

_____

_____

What I did with the rock: ☐ put it back

☐ saved for collection ☐ saved to give away

Other interesting things I noticed:

_____

_____

_____

_____

It looks like this (drawing or photo):

Fact

THE OLDEST ROCKS AND MINERALS ON EARTH

Many rocks have been around for millions of years, but the Earth is a lot older than that. It has been around for 4.5 billion years, and there aren't that many rocks still around from when the Earth was very young. In Australia, scientists have found a mineral called zircon that dates back to 4.3 billion years, long before any life existed on Earth.

Log

Date/Time:_____

City/State:_____

Rock location (in/near): ☐ lake ☐ mountain
☐ forest ☐ desert ☐ stream/river/creek
☐ other_____

Shape: ☐ mostly round ☐ mostly jagged
☐ other_____

Size: ☐ pea ☐ grape ☐ golf ball
☐ tennis ball ☐ larger or smaller, describe:
_____

Look/feel (check all that apply): ☐ rough
☐ smooth ☐ crystals ☐ banded ☐ veins
☐ layers ☐ pebbled ☐ grainy ☐ flaky
☐ holes/pockets ☐ other_____

Mostly metallic or metallic flecks/veins? If so,
describe:_____
_____

Color(s):_____
_____

Dull or shiny/glassy? Describe:_____
_____

Transparent or opaque? Describe:_____
_____

Type of rock/mineral I saw (enter this on your Life List)

Are there more of the same rock nearby?____

Describe the surrounding rocks/minerals:____

_____

_____

What I did with the rock: ☐ put it back
☐ saved for collection ☐ saved to give away

Other interesting things I noticed:

_____

_____

_____

_____

It looks like this (drawing or photo):

Fact

FOOL'S GOLD

If you found something golden and shiny on the ground, it means you've found gold, right? Not so fast. Fool's gold—also known as iron pyrite—is a lot more common than gold, but they both look a little bit alike. Once you look closer, fool's gold is a lot different: It's harder, has blocky crystal shapes (most gold is found in small flecks or lumps), and is far more common. But fool's gold is its own sort of treasure, as it's bright, pretty, and can even replace the minerals in fossils, creating bright, gold-colored fossils.

Log

Date/Time:_____

City/State:_____

Rock location (in/near): ☐ lake ☐ mountain
☐ forest ☐ desert ☐ stream/river/creek
☐ other_____

Shape: ☐ mostly round ☐ mostly jagged
☐ other_____

Size: ☐ pea ☐ grape ☐ golf ball
☐ tennis ball ☐ larger or smaller, describe:
_____

Look/feel (check all that apply): ☐ rough
☐ smooth ☐ crystals ☐ banded ☐ veins
☐ layers ☐ pebbled ☐ grainy ☐ flaky
☐ holes/pockets ☐ other_____

Mostly metallic or metallic flecks/veins? If so,
describe:_____
_____

Color(s):_____
_____

Dull or shiny/glassy? Describe:_____
_____

Transparent or opaque? Describe:_____
_____

Type of rock/mineral I saw (enter this on your Life List)

- Are there more of the same rock nearby?____
- Describe the surrounding rocks/minerals:____

_____

_____

What I did with the rock: ☐ put it back
☐ saved for collection ☐ saved to give away

Other interesting things I noticed:

_____

_____

_____

_____

It looks like this (drawing or photo):

Activity

ALPHA ROCKS

Figure out a word, name, phrase, or sentence you want to spell out on a rock.

Plan on one letter per rock or one word per rock, or fit the whole thing on one rock. Find the amount and type of rocks that you want.

Using acrylic paint and a paintbrush, or permanent marker, write those letters and words on the rock(s).

Put your new word art in your garden, on your bookshelf, or give it as a gift!

Log

Date/Time:_____

City/State:_____

Rock location (in/near): ☐ lake ☐ mountain
☐ forest ☐ desert ☐ stream/river/creek
☐ other_____

Shape: ☐ mostly round ☐ mostly jagged
☐ other_____

Size: ☐ pea ☐ grape ☐ golf ball
☐ tennis ball ☐ larger or smaller, describe:
_____

Look/feel (check all that apply): ☐ rough
☐ smooth ☐ crystals ☐ banded ☐ veins
☐ layers ☐ pebbled ☐ grainy ☐ flaky
☐ holes/pockets ☐ other_____

Mostly metallic or metallic flecks/veins? If so,
describe:_____
_____

Color(s):_____
_____

Dull or shiny/glassy? Describe:_____
_____

Transparent or opaque? Describe:_____
_____

Type of rock/mineral I saw (enter this on your Life List)

Are there more of the same rock nearby?____

Describe the surrounding rocks/minerals:____

_____

_____

What I did with the rock: ☐ put it back

☐ saved for collection ☐ saved to give away

Other interesting things I noticed:

_____

_____

_____

_____

It looks like this (drawing or photo):

Fact

GEODES: IT'S WHAT'S INSIDE THAT COUNTS

On the outside, geodes don't look like much, just round rocks. But when you crack them open—care-fully—you get a treat: geodes are hollow and filled with many tiny crystals. And until you open one up, you never know what's inside . . .

Note: If you find/ buy a geode, make sure you have an adult's help to open it up. The best way to do it is to put it into a sock or a plastic bag and hit it carefully with a hammer. Then it's just a matter of seeing what's inside.

Log

Date/Time:_____

City/State:_____

Rock location (in/near): ☐ lake ☐ mountain
☐ forest ☐ desert ☐ stream/river/creek
☐ other_____

Shape: ☐ mostly round ☐ mostly jagged
☐ other_____

Size: ☐ pea ☐ grape ☐ golf ball
☐ tennis ball ☐ larger or smaller, describe:
_____

Look/feel (check all that apply): ☐ rough
☐ smooth ☐ crystals ☐ banded ☐ veins
☐ layers ☐ pebbled ☐ grainy ☐ flaky
☐ holes/pockets ☐ other_____

Mostly metallic or metallic flecks/veins? If so,
describe:_____
_____

Color(s):_____
_____

Dull or shiny/glassy? Describe:_____
_____

Transparent or opaque? Describe:_____
_____

Type of rock/mineral I saw (enter this on your Life List)

Are there more of the same rock nearby?____

Describe the surrounding rocks/minerals:____

_____

_____

What I did with the rock: ☐ put it back
☐ saved for collection ☐ saved to give away

Other interesting things I noticed:

_____

_____

_____

_____

It looks like this (drawing or photo):

Fact

ROCKS FROM SPACE

Not all rocks found on Earth actually formed here. A few come from outer space.

Most rocks that fall to Earth burn up in the atmosphere, but some rocks are big enough to make it all the way down to the surface. They are called meteorites.

It is not easy to find a meteorite, but they are possible to find, if you study and look long and hard enough.

Log

Date/Time:_____

City/State:_____

Rock location (in/near): ☐ lake ☐ mountain
☐ forest ☐ desert ☐ stream/river/creek
☐ other_____

Shape: ☐ mostly round ☐ mostly jagged
☐ other_____

Size: ☐ pea ☐ grape ☐ golf ball
☐ tennis ball ☐ larger or smaller, describe:
_____

Look/feel (check all that apply): ☐ rough
☐ smooth ☐ crystals ☐ banded ☐ veins
☐ layers ☐ pebbled ☐ grainy ☐ flaky
☐ holes/pockets ☐ other_____

Mostly metallic or metallic flecks/veins? If so,
describe:_____
_____

Color(s):_____
_____

Dull or shiny/glassy? Describe:_____
_____

Transparent or opaque? Describe:_____
_____

Type of rock/mineral I saw (enter this on your Life List)

- Are there more of the same rock nearby?____
- Describe the surrounding rocks/minerals:____

_____

_____

What I did with the rock: ☐ put it back
☐ saved for collection ☐ saved to give away

Other interesting things I noticed:

_____

_____

_____

_____

It looks like this (drawing or photo):

Fact

SOAPSTONE

Soapstone is a metamorphic rock that gets its name because it feels soft, like soap.

It's mostly made up of the mineral talc, which is very soft and which you can break with your fingers.

Because soapstone is soft, it's easy to carve and has been used in everything from pots and pans to statues, decorations, and even kitchen countertops.

11

Log

Date/Time:_____

City/State:_____

Rock location (in/near): ☐ lake ☐ mountain
☐ forest ☐ desert ☐ stream/river/creek
☐ other_____

Shape: ☐ mostly round ☐ mostly jagged
☐ other_____

Size: ☐ pea ☐ grape ☐ golf ball
☐ tennis ball ☐ larger or smaller, describe:
_____

Look/feel (check all that apply): ☐ rough
☐ smooth ☐ crystals ☐ banded ☐ veins
☐ layers ☐ pebbled ☐ grainy ☐ flaky
☐ holes/pockets ☐ other_____

Mostly metallic or metallic flecks/veins? If so,
describe:_____
_____

Color(s):_____
_____

Dull or shiny/glassy? Describe:_____

Transparent or opaque? Describe:_____

Type of rock/mineral I saw (enter this on your Life List)

Are there more of the same rock nearby?____

Describe the surrounding rocks/minerals:____

_____

_____

What I did with the rock: ☐ put it back
☐ saved for collection ☐ saved to give away

Other interesting things I noticed:

_____

_____

_____

_____

It looks like this (drawing or photo):

Fact

YOUR SIDEWALK
CHALK USED TO
BE ALIVE!

Limestone is a
sedimentary rock
that forms when
certain kinds of
ocean life die
and settle on the
sea floor.

Chalk is a special
kind of limestone
and is made up of
the protective
plates of certain
kinds of algae.

Over time, big
piles of these
plates build up,
creating big
"beds" of chalk.
Some famous
landmarks are
even made
of chalk; one
example is the
White Cliffs of
Dover in England.
They are made
entirely of chalk!

Log

Date/Time:_____

City/State:_____

Rock location (in/near): ☐ lake ☐ mountain
☐ forest ☐ desert ☐ stream/river/creek
☐ other_____

Shape: ☐ mostly round ☐ mostly jagged
☐ other_____

Size: ☐ pea ☐ grape ☐ golf ball
☐ tennis ball ☐ larger or smaller, describe:
_____

Look/feel (check all that apply): ☐ rough
☐ smooth ☐ crystals ☐ banded ☐ veins
☐ layers ☐ pebbled ☐ grainy ☐ flaky
☐ holes/pockets ☐ other_____

Mostly metallic or metallic flecks/veins? If so,
describe:_____
_____

Color(s):_____
_____

Dull or shiny/glassy? Describe:_____
_____

Transparent or opaque? Describe:_____
_____

Type of rock/mineral I saw (enter this on your Life List)

Are there more of the same rock nearby?____

Describe the surrounding rocks/minerals:____

_____

_____

What I did with the rock: ☐ put it back

☐ saved for collection ☐ saved to give away

Other interesting things I noticed:

_____

_____

_____

It looks like this (drawing or photo):

Activity

STONE SCAVENGER HUNT

Set a timer for the amount of time you'd like to play (usually a minimum of 10 minutes)

Find as many rocks as you can in that time which match the following categories:

SHAPES: •flat •ball •round •square •cube •triangle •heart •oval •egg

COLORS: •gray •black •white •tan •blue •green •red •orange •yellow •pink •silver •gold

OTHER TYPES: •has crystals •has a hole •has layers •has a grainy look •has a really strange feature (shape, pattern, etc.)

37

Log

Date/Time:_____

City/State:_____

Rock location (in/near): ☐ lake ☐ mountain
☐ forest ☐ desert ☐ stream/river/creek
☐ other_____

Shape: ☐ mostly round ☐ mostly jagged
☐ other_____

Size: ☐ pea ☐ grape ☐ golf ball
☐ tennis ball ☐ larger or smaller, describe:
_____

Look/feel (check all that apply): ☐ rough
☐ smooth ☐ crystals ☐ banded ☐ veins
☐ layers ☐ pebbled ☐ grainy ☐ flaky
☐ holes/pockets ☐ other_____

Mostly metallic or metallic flecks/veins? If so,
describe:_____
_____

Color(s):_____
_____

Dull or shiny/glassy? Describe: _____
_____

Transparent or opaque? Describe:_____

Are there more of the same rock nearby?____

Describe the surrounding rocks/minerals:____

_____

_____

What I did with the rock: ☐ put it back

☐ saved for collection ☐ saved to give away

Other interesting things I noticed:

_____

_____

_____

_____

It looks like this (drawing or photo):

Fact

ALL ABOUT DIAMONDS

Diamonds are a special kind of the element carbon. Graphite, which makes up the lead in your pencil, is another form of carbon. Diamonds and graphite are different because diamonds formed deep within the Earth, where there's a lot of heat and pressure. This also made diamonds incredibly hard.

You're not likely to find diamonds on your own, unless you visit a place like Crater of Diamonds State Park in Arkansas, where you can dig for diamonds. If you're lucky enough to find one, you can even keep it!

Log

Date/Time:_____

City/State:_____

Rock location (in/near): ☐ lake ☐ mountain
☐ forest ☐ desert ☐ stream/river/creek
☐ other_____

Shape: ☐ mostly round ☐ mostly jagged
☐ other_____

Size: ☐ pea ☐ grape ☐ golf ball
☐ tennis ball ☐ larger or smaller, describe:
_____

Look/feel (check all that apply): ☐ rough
☐ smooth ☐ crystals ☐ banded ☐ veins
☐ layers ☐ pebbled ☐ grainy ☐ flaky
☐ holes/pockets ☐ other_____

Mostly metallic or metallic flecks/veins? If so,
describe:_____
_____

Color(s):_____
_____

Dull or shiny/glassy? Describe:_____
_____

Transparent or opaque? Describe:_____
_____

Type of rock/mineral I saw (enter this on your Life List)

Are there more of the same rock nearby?____

Describe the surrounding rocks/minerals:____

_____

_____

What I did with the rock: ☐ put it back
☐ saved for collection ☐ saved to give away

Other interesting things I noticed:

_____

_____

_____

_____

It looks like this (drawing or photo):

Fact

FLINT: ONE OF THE FIRST TOOLS

Flint is a hard sedimentary mineral that's special for a couple of reasons. A kind of quartz, it breaks in a circular shape, and the resulting pieces are very sharp. Also known as "chert," it's one of the most important minerals in human history. That's because people used it to make some of the first stone tools, including axes, scrapers and arrowheads. Flint is also important because it can be used to make fire; when struck against a piece of iron, it sparks, making it one of the first ways people made fire.

Log

Date/Time:_____

City/State:_____

Rock location (in/near): ☐ lake ☐ mountain
☐ forest ☐ desert ☐ stream/river/creek
☐ other_____

Shape: ☐ mostly round ☐ mostly jagged
☐ other_____

Size: ☐ pea ☐ grape ☐ golf ball
☐ tennis ball ☐ larger or smaller, describe:
_____

Look/feel (check all that apply): ☐ rough
☐ smooth ☐ crystals ☐ banded ☐ veins
☐ layers ☐ pebbled ☐ grainy ☐ flaky
☐ holes/pockets ☐ other_____

Mostly metallic or metallic flecks/veins? If so,
describe:_____
_____

Color(s):_____
_____

Dull or shiny/glassy? Describe:_____
_____

Transparent or opaque? Describe:_____
_____

Type of rock/mineral I saw (enter this on your Life List)

Are there more of the same rock nearby?____

Describe the surrounding rocks/minerals:____

_____

_____

What I did with the rock: ☐ put it back
☐ saved for collection ☐ saved to give away

Other interesting things I noticed:

_____

_____

_____

_____

It looks like this (drawing or photo):

Activity

GAMES OF STONE

Make your own playing pieces for TIC-TAC-TOE or CHECKERS. To do so, use acrylic paint or permanent marker to paint or write on stones.

TIC-TAC-TOE: Paint 5 stones with an "X" and 5 with an "O." Draw lines on a piece of paper or cardboard or in the sand to create a grid 3 squares across by 3 squares down for a total of 9 spaces to play.

CHECKERS: Paint 12 stones with one color and 12 with another. Create an 8x8 grid with alternating colored squares to play.

Log

Date/Time:_____

City/State:_____

Rock location (in/near): ☐ lake ☐ mountain
☐ forest ☐ desert ☐ stream/river/creek
☐ other_____

Shape: ☐ mostly round ☐ mostly jagged
☐ other_____

Size: ☐ pea ☐ grape ☐ golf ball
☐ tennis ball ☐ larger or smaller, describe:
_____

Look/feel (check all that apply): ☐ rough
☐ smooth ☐ crystals ☐ banded ☐ veins
☐ layers ☐ pebbled ☐ grainy ☐ flaky
☐ holes/pockets ☐ other_____

Mostly metallic or metallic flecks/veins? If so,
describe:_____
_____

Color(s):_____
_____

Dull or shiny/glassy? Describe:_____
_____

Transparent or opaque? Describe:_____
_____

Type of rock/mineral I saw (enter this on your Life List)

Are there more of the same rock nearby?____

Describe the surrounding rocks/minerals:____

_____

_____

What I did with the rock: ☐ put it back
☐ saved for collection ☐ saved to give away

Other interesting things I noticed:

_____

_____

_____

_____

It looks like this (drawing or photo):

Fact

QUARTZ: THE MOST COMMON MINERAL ON EARTH

Quartz is the most common mineral, occurring almost everywhere on Earth. In fact, if you've seen sand or landscaping rock, or used a smartphone, chances are you've seen some quartz today! Quartz is popular with rock collectors because it can form beautiful crystals and because it occurs in many colors. Purple quartz is known as "amethyst;" dark brown quartz is "smoky quartz," yellow quartz is "citrine." See if you can collect them all.

17

Log

Date/Time:_____

City/State:_____

Rock location (in/near): ☐ lake ☐ mountain
☐ forest ☐ desert ☐ stream/river/creek
☐ other_____

Shape: ☐ mostly round ☐ mostly jagged
☐ other_____

Size: ☐ pea ☐ grape ☐ golf ball
☐ tennis ball ☐ larger or smaller, describe:
_____

Look/feel (check all that apply): ☐ rough
☐ smooth ☐ crystals ☐ banded ☐ veins
☐ layers ☐ pebbled ☐ grainy ☐ flaky
☐ holes/pockets ☐ other_____

Mostly metallic or metallic flecks/veins? If so,
describe:_____
_____

Color(s):_____
_____

Dull or shiny/glassy? Describe:_____
_____

Transparent or opaque? Describe:_____
_____

Type of rock/mineral I saw (enter this on your Life List)

Are there more of the same rock nearby?____

Describe the surrounding rocks/minerals:____

_____

_____

What I did with the rock: ☐ put it back
☐ saved for collection ☐ saved to give away

Other interesting things I noticed:

_____

_____

_____

_____

It looks like this (drawing or photo):

Fact

GRANITE

Granite is a rock that forms deep within the Earth, where it is hot and there is a lot of pressure. How do we know? Well, when a volcano spits out hot lava and it cools off, it becomes a drab rock known as basalt. Basalt doesn't have visible crystals; that's because crystals are like plants; they need time (and the right conditions) to grow. Granite forms slowly, so its crystals had time to grow deep within the Earth. This is why it's so shiny and often used for things like kitchen countertops or tile floors.

Log

Date/Time:_____

City/State:_____

Rock location (in/near): ☐ lake ☐ mountain
☐ forest ☐ desert ☐ stream/river/creek
☐ other_____

Shape: ☐ mostly round ☐ mostly jagged
☐ other_____

Size: ☐ pea ☐ grape ☐ golf ball
☐ tennis ball ☐ larger or smaller, describe:
_____

Look/feel (check all that apply): ☐ rough
☐ smooth ☐ crystals ☐ banded ☐ veins
☐ layers ☐ pebbled ☐ grainy ☐ flaky
☐ holes/pockets ☐ other_____

Mostly metallic or metallic flecks/veins? If so,
describe:_____
_____

Color(s):_____
_____

Dull or shiny/glassy? Describe:_____
_____

Transparent or opaque? Describe:_____
_____

Type of rock/mineral I saw (enter this on your Life List)

- Are there more of the same rock nearby?____
- Describe the surrounding rocks/minerals:____

_____
_____

What I did with the rock: ☐ put it back
☐ saved for collection ☐ saved to give away

Other interesting things I noticed:

_____
_____
_____
_____

It looks like this (drawing or photo):

Fact

COPPER TURNING GREEN

Have you ever seen a penny or a statue that looked a little green? It was probably made of copper. Copper is a metal that is used in everything from electronics to statues. When exposed to oxygen, copper changes, forming a tarnish. This happens because two different chemicals are interacting. It's also why the Statue of Liberty, which is made out of copper, is now a light green. It used to be a dull copper color, but people liked the green so much the government decided to keep it.

Log

Date/Time:_____

City/State:_____

Rock location (in/near): ☐ lake ☐ mountain
☐ forest ☐ desert ☐ stream/river/creek
☐ other_____

Shape: ☐ mostly round ☐ mostly jagged
☐ other_____

Size: ☐ pea ☐ grape ☐ golf ball
☐ tennis ball ☐ larger or smaller, describe:
_____

Look/feel (check all that apply): ☐ rough
☐ smooth ☐ crystals ☐ banded ☐ veins
☐ layers ☐ pebbled ☐ grainy ☐ flaky
☐ holes/pockets ☐ other_____

Mostly metallic or metallic flecks/veins? If so,
describe:_____
_____

Color(s):_____
_____

Dull or shiny/glassy? Describe:_____
_____

Transparent or opaque? Describe:_____
_____

Type of rock/mineral I saw (enter this on your Life List)

Are there more of the same rock nearby?_____
Describe the surrounding rocks/minerals:_____
_____
_____

What I did with the rock: ☐ put it back
☐ saved for collection ☐ saved to give away

Other interesting things I noticed:
_____
_____
_____
_____

It looks like this (drawing or photo):

Fact

PETRIFIED WOOD

If the conditions are just right, a dead tree can turn to stone. For this to happen, it has to be covered with dirt or mud. As more dirt and debris piles on top, the tree becomes "locked in." Eventually, water and sand make their way into the tree and start to form crystals, replacing the original wood. The result is called petrified wood, and it's one of the most incredible rocks on Earth. There's even a famous national park—Petrified Wood National Park, in Arizona— where you can see huge trees made entirely out of brightly colored stone.

51

Log

Date/Time:_____

City/State:_____

Rock location (in/near): ☐ lake ☐ mountain
☐ forest ☐ desert ☐ stream/river/creek
☐ other_____

Shape: ☐ mostly round ☐ mostly jagged
☐ other_____

Size: ☐ pea ☐ grape ☐ golf ball
☐ tennis ball ☐ larger or smaller, describe:
_____

Look/feel (check all that apply): ☐ rough
☐ smooth ☐ crystals ☐ banded ☐ veins
☐ layers ☐ pebbled ☐ grainy ☐ flaky
☐ holes/pockets ☐ other_____

Mostly metallic or metallic flecks/veins? If so,
describe:_____
_____

Color(s):_____
_____

Dull or shiny/glassy? Describe:_____
_____

Transparent or opaque? Describe:_____
_____

Type of rock/mineral I saw (enter this on your Life List)

Are there more of the same rock nearby?____

Describe the surrounding rocks/minerals:____

_____

_____

What I did with the rock: ☐ put it back
☐ saved for collection ☐ saved to give away

Other interesting things I noticed:

_____

_____

_____

_____

It looks like this (drawing or photo):

Activity

SECRET IDENTITY

Play this game with 2 or more people.

Each person finds a special rock and notices its texture, shape, weight, and smell.

Put all of the rocks in a bucket, shoebox or a container and add extra until you have about 6-8 rocks.

Each person takes a turn with closed eyes and takes one rock out at a time to find their own rock by feel and smell.

No peeking!

Once the player finds their rock, they put it back in the pile for the next player to take their turn.

21

Log

Date/Time:_____

City/State:_____

Rock location (in/near): ☐ lake ☐ mountain
☐ forest ☐ desert ☐ stream/river/creek
☐ other_____

Shape: ☐ mostly round ☐ mostly jagged
☐ other_____

Size: ☐ pea ☐ grape ☐ golf ball
☐ tennis ball ☐ larger or smaller, describe:
_____

Look/feel (check all that apply): ☐ rough
☐ smooth ☐ crystals ☐ banded ☐ veins
☐ layers ☐ pebbled ☐ grainy ☐ flaky
☐ holes/pockets ☐ other_____

Mostly metallic or metallic flecks/veins? If so,
describe:_____
_____

Color(s):_____
_____

Dull or shiny/glassy? Describe:_____
_____

Transparent or opaque? Describe:_____
_____

Type of rock/mineral I saw (enter this on your Life List)

54

Are there more of the same rock nearby?____

Describe the surrounding rocks/minerals:____

_____

_____

What I did with the rock: ☐ put it back
☐ saved for collection ☐ saved to give away

Other interesting things I noticed:

_____

_____

_____

_____

It looks like this (drawing or photo):

Fact

WHEN LIGHTNING STRIKES SAND

Lightning occurs when electricity builds up in clouds. Sometimes lightning goes from one cloud to another, but it often strikes the ground. If lightning strikes a tree, it can start it on fire, and it can hurt or kill people. But when it strikes sand, it does something special. Sand is made of a combination of silicon and oxygen, and sand is the main ingredient in glass. When lightning strikes sand, it makes a long sandy tube of glass called a fulgurite, which is a fragile, popular collectible.

Log

Date/Time:_____

City/State:_____

Rock location (in/near): ☐ lake ☐ mountain
☐ forest ☐ desert ☐ stream/river/creek
☐ other_____

Shape: ☐ mostly round ☐ mostly jagged
☐ other_____

Size: ☐ pea ☐ grape ☐ golf ball
☐ tennis ball ☐ larger or smaller, describe:
_____

Look/feel (check all that apply): ☐ rough
☐ smooth ☐ crystals ☐ banded ☐ veins
☐ layers ☐ pebbled ☐ grainy ☐ flaky
☐ holes/pockets ☐ other_____

Mostly metallic or metallic flecks/veins? If so,
describe:_____
_____

Color(s):_____
_____

Dull or shiny/glassy? Describe:_____

Transparent or opaque? Describe:_____
_____

Type of rock/mineral I saw (enter this on your Life List)

Are there more of the same rock nearby?____

Describe the surrounding rocks/minerals:____

_____

_____

What I did with the rock: ☐ put it back
☐ saved for collection ☐ saved to give away

Other interesting things I noticed:

_____

_____

_____

_____

It looks like this (drawing or photo):

Fact

WANT TO HOLD SOME OLD LAVA? FIND SOME BASALT

When lava comes out of a volcano, it can be as hot as 2200 degrees, but when exposed to air, it cools down quickly. When it does, it turns into a number of different kinds of rocks, but one of the most common is called basalt. It's a gray, featureless rock that can be found all over the world. Sometimes, it's filled with holes that formed when gas bubbles got stuck in the rock as it cooled. So while it may not look like much now, when you find some, you can definitely say you've held lava!

Log

Date/Time:_____

City/State:_____

Rock location (in/near): ☐ lake ☐ mountain
☐ forest ☐ desert ☐ stream/river/creek
☐ other_____

Shape: ☐ mostly round ☐ mostly jagged
☐ other_____

Size: ☐ pea ☐ grape ☐ golf ball
☐ tennis ball ☐ larger or smaller, describe:
_____

Look/feel (check all that apply): ☐ rough
☐ smooth ☐ crystals ☐ banded ☐ veins
☐ layers ☐ pebbled ☐ grainy ☐ flaky
☐ holes/pockets ☐ other_____

Mostly metallic or metallic flecks/veins? If so,
describe:_____
_____

Color(s):_____
_____

Dull or shiny/glassy? Describe:_____
_____

Transparent or opaque? Describe:_____
_____

Type of rock/mineral I saw (enter this on your Life List)

Are there more of the same rock nearby?____

Describe the surrounding rocks/minerals:____

_____

_____

What I did with the rock: ☐ put it back
☐ saved for collection ☐ saved to give away

Other interesting things I noticed:

_____

_____

_____

_____

It looks like this (drawing or photo):

Activity

STACKING ROCKS

Also called rock balancing, this is a great skill to learn.

Choose a base rock and several others. Try to find some with a scoop, a hole, or a flat space to balance another rock on top of it.

Take your time. Try different rock shapes and sizes. See how high you can stack or how unusual your creation can be.

Make an inukshuk; this is a rock stack that looks like a person.

Early native people in Canada used them as signs to mark directions or even on gravesites.

Log

Date/Time:_____

City/State:_____

Rock location (in/near): ☐ lake ☐ mountain
☐ forest ☐ desert ☐ stream/river/creek
☐ other_____

Shape: ☐ mostly round ☐ mostly jagged
☐ other_____

Size: ☐ pea ☐ grape ☐ golf ball
☐ tennis ball ☐ larger or smaller, describe:
_____

Look/feel (check all that apply): ☐ rough
☐ smooth ☐ crystals ☐ banded ☐ veins
☐ layers ☐ pebbled ☐ grainy ☐ flaky
☐ holes/pockets ☐ other_____

Mostly metallic or metallic flecks/veins? If so,
describe:_____
_____

Color(s):_____
_____

Dull or shiny/glassy? Describe:_____
_____

Transparent or opaque? Describe:_____
_____

Type of rock/mineral I saw (enter this on your Life List)

Are there more of the same rock nearby?____

Describe the surrounding rocks/minerals:____

_____

_____

What I did with the rock: ☐ put it back
☐ saved for collection ☐ saved to give away

Other interesting things I noticed:

_____

_____

_____

_____

It looks like this (drawing or photo):

Fact

MARBLE VS. LEMON JUICE

Marble is a hard metamorphic rock that contains calcium, a chemical element that reacts (or changes) when exposed to acids. For centuries, marble has been used in buildings, countertops, statues, and even headstones for graves. But marble can be damaged by acids, including those found in lemon juice, vinegar, or even soft drinks. When exposed to such acids, marble starts to bubble and can even change colors. Rain, which can be acidic due to pollution, is another threat to marble.

Log

Date/Time:_____

City/State:_____

Rock location (in/near): ☐ lake ☐ mountain
☐ forest ☐ desert ☐ stream/river/creek
☐ other_____

Shape: ☐ mostly round ☐ mostly jagged
☐ other_____

Size: ☐ pea ☐ grape ☐ golf ball
☐ tennis ball ☐ larger or smaller, describe:
_____

Look/feel (check all that apply): ☐ rough
☐ smooth ☐ crystals ☐ banded ☐ veins
☐ layers ☐ pebbled ☐ grainy ☐ flaky
☐ holes/pockets ☐ other_____

Mostly metallic or metallic flecks/veins? If so,
describe:_____
_____

Color(s):_____
_____

Dull or shiny/glassy? Describe:_____
_____

Transparent or opaque? Describe:_____
_____

Type of rock/mineral I saw (enter this on your Life List)

Are there more of the same rock nearby?____

Describe the surrounding rocks/minerals:____

_____

_____

What I did with the rock: ☐ put it back
☐ saved for collection ☐ saved to give away

Other interesting things I noticed:

_____

_____

_____

_____

It looks like this (drawing or photo):

Fact

GOLD

People have loved gold for thousands of years. Popular in jewelry and long used as money, gold also has important uses in technology, especially in laptops, phones, and tablets. If you want to find gold, you'll probably have to work at a mine, but many rock shops have vials of gold flakes that you can buy, and many tourist sites give kids the opportunity to pan for gold. Don't expect to strike it rich, though: gold is unique because a small amount can be stretched out a lot, so any gold "flakes" you find may look big, but there isn't really much gold there at all.

Log

Date/Time:_____

City/State:_____

Rock location (in/near): ☐ lake ☐ mountain
☐ forest ☐ desert ☐ stream/river/creek
☐ other_____

Shape: ☐ mostly round ☐ mostly jagged
☐ other_____

Size: ☐ pea ☐ grape ☐ golf ball
☐ tennis ball ☐ larger or smaller, describe:
_____

Look/feel (check all that apply): ☐ rough
☐ smooth ☐ crystals ☐ banded ☐ veins
☐ layers ☐ pebbled ☐ grainy ☐ flaky
☐ holes/pockets ☐ other_____

Mostly metallic or metallic flecks/veins? If so,
describe:_____
_____

Color(s):_____
_____

Dull or shiny/glassy? Describe:_____
_____

Transparent or opaque? Describe:_____
_____

Type of rock/mineral I saw (enter this on your Life List)

- Are there more of the same rock nearby?____
- Describe the surrounding rocks/minerals:____

_____
_____

What I did with the rock: ☐ put it back
☐ saved for collection ☐ saved to give away

Other interesting things I noticed:

_____
_____
_____
_____

It looks like this (drawing or photo):

Activity

RAINBOW ROCKS

Find smooth rocks in shapes and sizes that you like.

Spread glue on a rock—tacky glue or white glue spread thinly will both work well. Paste does not work at all.

Start at one end, wrapping the rock with various yarns, embroidery floss, or colored strings, working your way around the rock to the other end.

Change colors or type of string as often as you like while you're wrapping.

Make more of these in many sizes for a custom rainbow rock collection!

Log

Date/Time:_____

City/State:_____

Rock location (in/near): ☐ lake ☐ mountain
☐ forest ☐ desert ☐ stream/river/creek
☐ other_____

Shape: ☐ mostly round ☐ mostly jagged
☐ other_____

Size: ☐ pea ☐ grape ☐ golf ball
☐ tennis ball ☐ larger or smaller, describe:
_____

Look/feel (check all that apply): ☐ rough
☐ smooth ☐ crystals ☐ banded ☐ veins
☐ layers ☐ pebbled ☐ grainy ☐ flaky
☐ holes/pockets ☐ other_____

Mostly metallic or metallic flecks/veins? If so,
describe:_____
_____

Color(s):_____
_____

Dull or shiny/glassy? Describe:_____
_____

Transparent or opaque? Describe:_____
_____

Type of rock/mineral I saw (enter this on your Life List)

Are there more of the same rock nearby?____
Describe the surrounding rocks/minerals:____

_____
_____

What I did with the rock: ☐ put it back
☐ saved for collection ☐ saved to give away

Other interesting things I noticed:

_____
_____
_____
_____

It looks like this (drawing or photo):

Fact

ROCKS THAT
GLOW IN
THE DARK

Some rocks don't
look like much, in
the daytime at
least. They're
drab and pretty
unexciting.

But if you turn out
the lights and shine
an ultraviolet light
(a special kind
of light people
can't see) on it,
the stones glow
in bright, strange
colors. This
happens because
the rocks and
minerals absorb
the ultraviolet
light and then
release a little bit
of visible light in
the process.
This is called
fluorescence. The
most famous type
of mineral that
lights up is called
fluorite; it glows in
a brilliant blue.

Log

Date/Time:_____

City/State:_____

Rock location (in/near): ☐ lake ☐ mountain
☐ forest ☐ desert ☐ stream/river/creek
☐ other_____

Shape: ☐ mostly round ☐ mostly jagged
☐ other_____

Size: ☐ pea ☐ grape ☐ golf ball
☐ tennis ball ☐ larger or smaller, describe:
_____

Look/feel (check all that apply): ☐ rough
☐ smooth ☐ crystals ☐ banded ☐ veins
☐ layers ☐ pebbled ☐ grainy ☐ flaky
☐ holes/pockets ☐ other_____

Mostly metallic or metallic flecks/veins? If so,
describe:_____
_____

Color(s):_____
_____

Dull or shiny/glassy? Describe:_____
_____

Transparent or opaque? Describe:_____
_____

Type of rock/mineral I saw (enter this on your Life List)

Are there more of the same rock nearby?____

Describe the surrounding rocks/minerals:____

_____

_____

What I did with the rock: ☐ put it back
☐ saved for collection ☐ saved to give away

Other interesting things I noticed:

_____

_____

_____

_____

It looks like this (drawing or photo):

Fact

AGATE

Agates are a special kind of the mineral chalcedony (kal-sed-o-knee) and famous for their colorful bands and lines. Agates are found all over the world, with many places in the United States famous for their own varieties. One of the most famous kinds of agate is the Lake Superior agate, found mostly in the Upper Midwest, especially in Minnesota, Wisconsin, and Michigan. It often has bright red or yellow bands, Wherever they are found, agate collecting is a fun way to learn about rocks and find some treasures to bring home.

Log

Date/Time:_____

City/State:_____

Rock location (in/near): ☐ lake ☐ mountain
☐ forest ☐ desert ☐ stream/river/creek
☐ other_____

Shape: ☐ mostly round ☐ mostly jagged
☐ other_____

Size: ☐ pea ☐ grape ☐ golf ball
☐ tennis ball ☐ larger or smaller, describe:
_____

Look/feel (check all that apply): ☐ rough
☐ smooth ☐ crystals ☐ banded ☐ veins
☐ layers ☐ pebbled ☐ grainy ☐ flaky
☐ holes/pockets ☐ other_____

Mostly metallic or metallic flecks/veins? If so,
describe:_____
_____

Color(s):_____
_____

Dull or shiny/glassy? Describe:_____
_____

Transparent or opaque? Describe:_____
_____

Type of rock/mineral I saw (enter this on your Life List)

Are there more of the same rock nearby?____

Describe the surrounding rocks/minerals:____

_____

_____

What I did with the rock: ☐ put it back
☐ saved for collection ☐ saved to give away

Other interesting things I noticed:

_____

_____

_____

_____

It looks like this (drawing or photo):

Activity

SANDY SURPRISE

Create a layered sand bottle.

Each time you visit a place that has sand, put a scoop of it—enough to create a 1/4-inch to 1-inch layer in a clear glass or plastic bottle. (But before taking any sand, make sure you have permission to do so.)

Place a piece of tape on the bottle from the top to the bottom. Draw a line on the tape where each layer ends. Then, with a permanent marker, write the location and date that you got each of the layers of sand.

Then put your sand art on display!

Log

Date/Time:_____

City/State:_____

Rock location (in/near): ☐ lake ☐ mountain
☐ forest ☐ desert ☐ stream/river/creek
☐ other_____

Shape: ☐ mostly round ☐ mostly jagged
☐ other_____

Size: ☐ pea ☐ grape ☐ golf ball
☐ tennis ball ☐ larger or smaller, describe:
_____

Look/feel (check all that apply): ☐ rough
☐ smooth ☐ crystals ☐ banded ☐ veins
☐ layers ☐ pebbled ☐ grainy ☐ flaky
☐ holes/pockets ☐ other_____

Mostly metallic or metallic flecks/veins? If so,
describe:_____
_____

Color(s):_____
_____

Dull or shiny/glassy? Describe:_____
_____

Transparent or opaque? Describe:_____
_____

Type of rock/mineral I saw (enter this on your Life List)

Are there more of the same rock nearby?____

Describe the surrounding rocks/minerals:____

_____

_____

What I did with the rock: ☐ put it back
☐ saved for collection ☐ saved to give away

Other interesting things I noticed:

_____

_____

_____

_____

It looks like this (drawing or photo):

Fact

RARE-EARTH MINERALS

Rare-earth elements get their name because they are only found in large amounts in a few places on Earth. This means that only a few countries have large amounts of them. They aren't exactly rare, though; gold is much rarer than any of the rare-earth elements. Rare-earth elements are used in a wide variety of electronic devices, including phones, computers, tablets, and more. This makes them important! Your smart phone or video games wouldn't work without them.

Photo/Art

Date: _____ Description: _____

_____

Photo/Art

Date: _____ Description: _____

_____

Photo/Art

Date: _____ Description: _____
_____

Photo/Art

Date: _____ Description: _____

_____

Photo/Art

Date: _____ Description: _____
_____

Color

Date:_____

Artist's Signature:_____

Color

Date:_____

Artist's Signature:_____